Presented By
Scripture Press Ministries
Glen Ellyn, Illinois, USA

Matthew 1-14

KENNETH O. GANGEL

VICTOR BOOKS®
A DIVISION OF SCRIPTURE PRESS PUBLICATIONS INC.
USA CANADA ENGLAND

Unless otherwise noted, Scripture quotations in this Bible study are from the *Holy Bible, New International Version,* © 1973, 1978, 1984, International Bible Society. Used by permission of Zondervan Bible Publishers.

Recommended Dewey Decimal Classification: 226.2
Suggested Subject Heading: BIBLE, N.T.—MATTHEW

Library of Congress Catalog Card Number: 87-62473
ISBN: 0-89693-459-4

©1988 by SP Publications, Inc. All rights reserved. Printed in the United States of America. No part of this book may be reproduced without written permission, except for brief quotations in books, critical articles, and reviews.

VICTOR BOOKS
A division of SP Publications, Inc.
Wheaton, Illinois 60187

CONTENTS

How to Use This Study   *7*
Introduction to the Gospel of Matthew   *9*

1. **MATTHEW 1** *Messiahship of the King*   *13*

2. **MATTHEW 2** *Manifestation of the King*   *19*

3. **MATTHEW 3** *Messenger of the King*   *25*

4. **MATTHEW 4** *Measure of the King*   *31*

5. **MATTHEW 5** *Message of the King—Part 1*   *37*

6. **MATTHEW 6** *Message of the King—Part 2*   *43*

7. **MATTHEW 7** *Message of the King—Part 3*   *49*

8. **MATTHEW 8—9** *Miracles of the King*   *57*

9. **MATTHEW 10** *Men of the King*   *63*

10. **MATTHEW 11—12** *Magnitude of the King*   *71*

11. **MATTHEW 13:1-52** *Mystery Reign of the King*   *79*

12. **MATTHEW 13:53—14:36** *Motives of the King*   *87*

How to Use This Study

Personal Growth Bible Studies are designed to help you understand God's Word and how it applies to everyday life. To complete the studies in this book, you will need to use a Bible. A good modern translation of the Bible, such as the *New International Version* or the *New American Standard Bible*, will give you the most help. (NOTE: the questions in this book are based on the *New International Version.*)

You will find it helpful to follow a similar sequence with each study. First, read the introductory paragraphs. This material helps set the tone and lay the groundwork for the passage to be studied. Once you have completed this part of the study, spend time reading the assigned passage in your Bible. This will give you a general feel for the contents of the passage.

Having completed the preliminaries, you are then ready to dig deeper into the Scripture passage. Each study is divided into several sections so that you can take a close-up look at the smaller parts of the larger passage. These sections each begin with a synopsis of the Scripture to be studied in that section. Following each synopsis is a two-part study section made up of *Explaining the Text* and *Examining the Text.*

Explaining the Text gives background notes and commentary to help you understand points in the text that may not be readily apparent. After reading any comments that appear in *Explaining the Text*, answer each question under *Examining the Text.*

At the end of each study is a section called *Experiencing the Text.* The questions in this section focus on the application of biblical principles to life. You may find that some of the questions can be answered immediately; others will require that you spend more time reflecting on the passages you have just studied.

The distinctive format of the Personal Growth Bible Studies makes them easy to use individually as well as for group study. If the majority of those in your group answer the questions before the group meeting, spend most of your time together discussing the *Experiencing* questions.

If, on the other hand, members have not answered the questions ahead of time and you have adequate time in your group meeting, work through all of the questions together.

However you use this series of studies, our prayer is that you will understand the Bible as never before, and that because of this understanding, you will experience a rich and dynamic Christian life. If questions of interpretation arise in the course of this study, we recommend you refer to the two-volume set, *The Bible Knowledge Commentary*, edited by John F. Walvoord and Roy B. Zuck (Victor Books, 1984, 1986).

Introduction to the Gospel of Matthew

Sometime after the dispersion of the Jerusalem church, yet probably before the year A.D. 70 when Jerusalem was destroyed, Matthew penned his dramatic history of the life of Christ which we now recognize as the first book of the New Testament. Scholars believe the original manuscript may have been written in Aramaic, but was quickly replaced by a Greek edition, perhaps written by the author himself.

Though the author is not identified in the book, Eusebius and Irenaeus both credit the book to Matthew, and few scholars have ever disputed Matthew's authorship, though he disappears from church history after a brief mention in Acts 1:13.

Matthew obviously intended to first prove to Jews who were already familiar with Old Testament prophecies that Jesus of Nazareth was the Messiah (Christ). Secondly, he wanted to explain to any Gentiles who might read his book how the Old Testament was fulfilled and explained in Christ.

The name Matthew means "gift of God," and more space is given in this Gospel than any other to Jesus' teaching ministry, making it about 60 percent of Matthew's content. The word *church* is found in this Gospel alone, and according to A.T. Robertson, Matthew quotes from the Old Testament 93 times, mentioning the kingdom of heaven at least 33 times. In fact, the key words in this Gospel are "king" and "kingdom."

As we study the first 14 chapters of the book, may the Spirit of God produce in our hearts not only an awareness of the Messiah but a conscious experience of His presence in our lives.

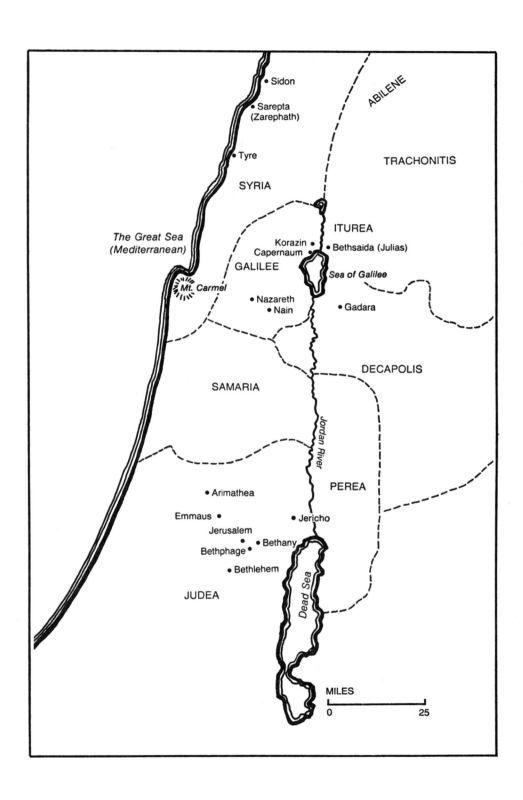

STUDY ONE
Matthew 1

Messiahship of the King

The New Testament opens with Rome ruling the world. Roman peace, Roman law, and Roman roads, developed in the providence of God, prepared the world for the coming of the Messiah. The fullness of time had come.

Nevertheless, the empire of Alexander the Great lived on in Greek culture called "Hellenism." Rather than destroying Greek culture, Rome absorbed it so that the literature, philosophy, arts, and language of the day were commonly Greek. There was even a Greek version of the Old Testament called the Septuagint.

In many ways these days (approximately 4 b.c.) were brighter than the centuries which had gone before. Yet life was cheap and sin was rampant. Throughout the later days of the Old Testament the Jews were dispersed throughout Assyria and Babylonia. Though they took the religion of Moses to foreign lands, they also brought back foreign culture and ideas to Palestine. Local synagogues sprang up all over the Mediterranean world, and thousands of Gentiles became proselytes of Judaism. Among many, messianic expectancy was high. In such a setting of dramatic suspense, God sent a Saviour.

A. BACKGROUND OF THE MESSIAH (*Matt. 1:1-17*). Genealogies are extremely important to Jews because of their strong sense of nationalism. Add that to the author's background setting of the King, and the record of the Messiah's birth becomes essential—He must be of a royal bloodline. The genealogy of these verses records Joseph's connection with David which comes through Solomon, while Luke traces Mary's link to David through Nathan. Where did the information in these opening chapters come from? Perhaps from Joseph himself.

Examining the Text

1. Read Matthew 1:1-17. Most people who study the Bible think genealogies are unimportant and certainly uninteresting. In addition to the royal line argument, list some reasons why God would choose to start the New Testament with a genealogy.

2. Examine the names that Matthew lists and see if you can arrange them into three divisions.

3. Why would God lead Matthew to include some wicked kings in his genealogy?

Explaining the Text

1. As you read through this genealogy, note that the words *father of* do not necessarily mean immediate generation but direct generation. It is not the author's purpose to name every individual in the entire line, but to show the direct connection between Jesus and David.

2. Unlike Matthew's genealogy in these verses, Luke's record lists 76 names. Luke also includes 20 names prior to Abraham. Remember Matthew's purpose—to establish the legal and regal authority of Jesus the King. Luke, on the other hand, wished to emphasize the appeal of the Gospel for Gentiles.

3. Obviously several names have been left out of Matthew's genealogy. In verse 8, after Jehoram, three names are omitted—Ahaziah, Joash, and Amaziah. Most commentators agree they were dropped because all were descendants of the

Explaining the Text	*Examining the Text*
wicked Queen Athaliah and belonged to a very dark period of Israel's history.	
	4. The principle of progressive revelation states that God reveals His truth to us a little at a time as we are able to receive it. How does that principle show up in the first 17 verses of Matthew 1?
	5. Carefully study verse 16. Why is the wording of this verse different from all the verses which come before it in this chapter?
6. The answer to the Jeconiah curse is the Virgin Birth protected by the wording of verse 16. The Scriptures do not tell us that Joseph was "the father of Jesus" though that would have been the normal wording in line with the rest of the chapter. The Virgin Birth is the way God gets around the curse on Jeconiah and legitimately offers the throne to His Son Jesus.	6. Other than clear title to the throne, why is the doctrine of the Virgin Birth important to Christians today?

B. BIRTH OF THE MESSIAH (*Matt. 1:18-25*). The second half of Matthew's first chapter offers a special look at a special couple. Joseph, a righteous, sensitive, and obedient Jew, responds immediately to God's involvement in his life. Matthew's record of Jesus' birth is brief because, unlike Luke, he is unconcerned with historic details. He has already established the royal line, and now he merely wants to emphasize the miraculous nature of the way God sent the Messiah into the world. The first two sections teach us about the agony of Joseph when he learns of Mary's pregnancy. Verses 20 and 21 describe the family while the final four verses explain the fulfillment of prophecy.

Examining the Text	*Explaining the Text*
1. Read Matthew 1:18-25. The text tells us Joseph "had in mind to divorce her quietly" (v. 19). How and why would he do this?	1. Betrothal or engagement among the Jews was a sacred ritual, far more binding than anything we know today. Notice the word *husband* is used even before the marriage (v. 19). Not only was engagement a sacred ritual of the Jews of the first century but the law called for death in cases of fornication (Deut. 22:21).
2. How did the angel address Joseph, and how do you think he might have responded?	
3. Use a Bible dictionary to find out the meaning of the name Jesus.	3. In all of history God has formed human beings in only four ways—from the dust of the ground (Adam), from man without woman (Eve), from woman without man (Christ), and natural, ordinary procreation of man and woman together.
4. To what is Matthew referring in verse 23? Use your concordance if necessary.	

Messiahship of the King

Explaining the Text	*Examining the Text*
5. Matthew tells us Joseph had "no union" with Mary until after Jesus was born (v. 25). Nothing was to interfere with the supernatural Virgin Birth. In later chapters of Matthew, we will discover that other children were naturally born to this couple after the birth of Jesus.	5. List at least three specific ways that Joseph was obedient to the angel's command.

Experiencing the Text

1. Tamar, Rahab, and Ruth are listed in the genealogy of Christ in verses 3 and 5. What practical significance do you see in this inclusion?

2. Matthew works hard in this chapter to establish the royal bloodline of the Messiah. Name some modern situations in which bloodline or ancestor relationships are important.

3. We talk a lot about making Jesus King in our lives. In what specific way can you do that?

4. List at least four practical spiritual lessons from these 17 verses of genealogy.

5. Briefly compare Joseph's response to Mary's pregnancy with modern attitudes on divorce.

6. What spiritual lessons can you learn from Joseph's handling of this crisis?

7. Suppose you are a Sunday School teacher of third graders and you are assigned Matthew 1:1-17. How would you teach it? What would you emphasize?

8. This chapter of Matthew ends with the words "the name Jesus." Are there any special ways we should use the name of Jesus today?

9. Notice the significance of worship in this chapter (v. 23). Linking with the words of Jesus in John 4:24, list some ways you can worship the Lord in private, apart from church services and formal gatherings.

STUDY TWO
Matthew 2

Manifestation of the King

Kings are not always recognizable. Peter the Second, the last king of Yugoslavia, died of pneumonia in Los Angeles after working as a savings and loan executive in that city during the last years of his life. He was 11 years old when his father was assassinated in 1934, and seven years later he took full control of the government from a council of regents, leading a brief campaign against Nazi invaders before fleeing to Britain. He was formally deposed by the Tito government in 1945 and eventually made his way to the United States.

Matthew tells us how God conducted an astronomical manifestation of the coming of His king. With the Heavenly Father in control of every detail, an entire nation was disrupted.

A. REVERENCE OF THE KING BY THE MAGI (*Matt. 2:1-12*). Matthew almost sounds like Luke as he opens his second chapter with the phrase "during the time of King Herod" (v. 1). Herod the Great died in 4 B.C., so we know the birth of Christ was either in that year or shortly before it.

These 12 verses tell us about the worship of the mysterious group of people called "magi" or wise men. They break upon the scene and then disappear, never to be heard of again. Perhaps the mystery compels us to build myths around these foreign worshipers. But our study will deal only with what the text tells us.

Examining the Text	*Explaining the Text*
1. Read Matthew 2:1-12. Tradition aside, what specific information do we have about the wise men?	1. Every Christmas scene has shepherds and wise men kneeling together at the manger in Bethlehem. More likely the wise men came later since Scripture tells us they visited the child in a house.
2. Notice how Herod reacted to the message of the Magi. How do you account for his response?	2. Herod the Great was not the rightful king from the line of David. He was descended from Esau and reigned over Palestine from 37–4 B.C. A pragmatic vassal of Rome, Herod was hated by most of the Jews he ruled.
3. Study carefully Matthew's appeal to prophecy in verses 5-6. Why is the accuracy of the Bethlehem account so important?	3. Astronomers tell us that the universe contains at least 12 quadrillion solar systems, each containing billions of stars. But this one was different. A supernatural phenomenon appeared in the East and guided these worshipers to the unlikely town of Bethlehem.

B. RESCUE OF THE KING THROUGH DIVINE INTERVENTION (*Matt. 2:13-18*). In fulfillment of Hosea 11:1, God, through His angel, sends the little family to Egypt. Again we see examples of Joseph's obedience and a graphic picture of the maniacal rule of Herod the Great. According to Josephus, Herod died as his body was rotting, consumed by worms. His grandson, Herod Agrippa, died a similar death (Acts 12:23).

Explaining the Text	*Examining the Text*
1. Satan attempted to halt the work of the Messiah, but God overruled him by sending yet another angelic message to Joseph.	1. Read Matthew 2:13-18. Count the number of times the angels spoke to Joseph in Matthew 1–2.
2. Herod's order to kill all the boys in Bethlehem and its vicinity who were two years old and under fulfilled the prophecy of Jeremiah 31:15-16. The initial application of the prophecy focused on the deaths of children at the time of the Babylonian captivity, and in both instances, Rachel represents grieving mothers of Israel.	2. Couldn't the God who arranged the Virgin Birth prevent this slaughter? Why do you think He allowed Herod a free hand to murder so viciously?
	3. From the information available in this chapter, list three points of contrast between King Jesus and King Herod.

C. RETURN OF THE KING TO NAZARETH (*Matt. 2:19-23*). Several times already we have noted that Matthew's writing is geared to his purpose—to present the Messiah as King. He does not wish to write a complete biography, but to focus specifically on those aspects of the birth, childhood, and ministry of Christ which relate to messiahship. Consequently, in these last two paragraphs of the chapter, the author records the family's return from Egypt to settle in the town of Nazareth.

Examining the Text

1. Read Matthew 2:19-23. Find a good Bible atlas and locate Nazareth, noting particularly its relationship to Bethelehem, Jerusalem, and Egypt.

2. Verse 23 connects "Nazareth" and "Nazarene." Numbers 6:1-21 carries a different idea. Study that passage and identify the difference.

Explaining the Text

1. Herod the Great had been replaced by his son, Archelaus, who started his reign by murdering about 3,000 people for political reasons. Obviously, things were not going to be any better in Judea, so Joseph headed north to Galilee.

2. Commentators can't agree about the reference to a "Nazarene" at the end of this chapter. Possibly Matthew had in mind Isaiah 11:1 with its reference to the branch (*netzer*) and somehow connected that with the city of Nazareth.

Experiencing the Text

1. A bumper sticker commonly seen in America over the past few years reads, "Wise men still seek Him." Historically it refers to our chapter; but what does it mean for today?

2. The wise men came to find the Messiah. Can you think of any world rulers today who are looking for the Messiah, or recognize that He has already come?

Manifestation of the King

3. Think of ways the record of the wise men has been distorted in Christmas celebrations at your church. How might this be corrected?

4. Was Herod's murder of the children an example of satanic intervention? How does Satan work today to try to thwart and upset the plans of God?

5. Does God still speak to people in dreams?

6. Why would it have been hard for people of Jesus' time to immediately recognize Him as the Messiah?

7. What evidence of Jesus' life and ministry have helped you recognize Him as the Messiah?

STUDY THREE
Matthew 3

Messenger of the King

John the Baptist appeared on the scene of the New Testament as a human bridge between the old and new covenants. At the same time, he served as an Old Testament prophet committed to the Law and a New Testament saint stretching out to reach the grace of the Saviour.

How does the Bible describe John the Baptist? Jesus said of him, "I tell you the truth: among those born of women there has not risen anyone greater than John the Baptist" (Matt. 11:11). Yet of himself, John testifies, "A man can receive only what is given him from heaven. You yourselves can testify that I said, 'I am not the Christ but am sent ahead of Him.' The bride belongs to the bridegroom. The friend who attends the bridegroom waits and listens for him, and is full of joy when he hears the bridegroom's voice. That joy is mine, and it is now complete. He must become greater; I must become less" (John 3:27-30).

This lesson focuses not just on the Baptizer but also the baptism. Why did it occur? Why at this time? Why in this manner? These are some of the questions before us as we allow the Holy Spirit to instruct us in the message of our chapter.

A. THE MESSENGER (*Matt. 3:1-4*). Matthew's announcement of the preacher stands in direct connection with his ministry as a messianic forerunner. Remember Matthew's camera is carefully focused on the King, and the people around the King only come into peripheral vision. Nevertheless, the Spirit of God directs the Gospel writer to draw a continuous parallel between Elijah and John. And in the first four verses of chapter 3, we see a fascinating assemblage of pictures—full-color, literary Polaroid shots of one of the unique characters in the New Testament.

Examining the Text	*Explaining the Text*
1. Read Matthew 3:1-4. How would you describe from these verses the central theme of John's message?	1. The word *repent* literally means to change one's purpose or to turn around and walk in a different direction.
2. Why do you think Matthew quotes Isaiah 40:3 in introducing John the Baptist to his readers?	
3. What does this passage tell us about the character and personality of John?	3. Some scholars identify John the Baptist with a sect known as the Essenes. Though he certainly seems like one of these zealots in many ways, there seems to be little proof of that connection.

Messenger of the King

B. THE MESSAGE (*Matt. 3:5-12*). The great British expositor G. Campbell Morgan liked to say that John's ministry was attractive (many went out to meet him), convictive (many responded and were baptized), and invective (it contained a clarion protest against the Pharisees and Sadducees). This section describes John's congregation, his conflict with religious legalists, and his clear prophecy of the conquest of the King.

Explaining the Text	*Examining the Text*
1. Israel had not heard the voice of a prophet for 400 years. After centuries of revolt, religious confusion, and scrolls of rabbinical tradition gathering dust in synagogues across the land, the desert suddenly echoes with the electrifying voice of a man who seems to speak for God. Small wonder crowds gathered by the Jordan.	1. Read Matthew 3:5-12. On a map of Palestine during this time period, locate all the geographical references in these four verses.
	2. How many times does the concept of fire appear in these verses? Do you have an explanation of why John refers to this so frequently?
3. John was an Old Testament prophet calling people to repentance and preparation for the coming of the Messiah. The baptism of the New Testament practiced after the Resurrection and Pentecost recognized that the Messiah had already come, died, and risen again.	3. Note the strong emphasis on the wrath of God. What is there about this preaching situation which seems to require that kind of emphasis from John?

C. THE MESSIAH (*Matt. 3:13-17*). Matthew wants us to understand the baptism of Jesus as more than a historical event. The record of God's voice attending the occasion invokes the attention of the world upon the ministry of the King. John and other devout Jews present that day may very well have thought of Psalm 2 in which Jehovah promised that the pagan rulers of the world would never stand against the power and glory of the Messiah.

Examining the Text	*Explaining the Text*
1. Read Matthew 3:13-17. Check your atlas again. How did Jesus get to where John ministered, and why was He coming from Galilee?	
2. List several reasons why John at first refused to baptize Jesus.	
3. The baptism of Christ seems to have fulfilled several purposes in the plan of God. Identify several.	3. Someone has described the dove as the "lamb of the birds," the poorest of Old Testament sacrifices.
4. Locate evidence that all three Persons of the Trinity were present at the baptism of Jesus.	4. The events of verse 16 are a fulfillment of Isaiah 11:2, where the prophet indicates that God's Spirit will rest on the Messiah.

Messenger of the King

Experiencing the Text

1. Write some names of other people in the history of the church who carried out roles similar to the one God gave John the Baptist.

2. How is repentance related to faith? To conversion?

3. Think about the attitudes of your congregation for just a moment. How do they (and you) respond to people who dress and act differently?

4. In modern-day terms, name some "fruit in keeping with repentance" (v. 8).

5. What are the requirements and procedures for baptism at your church?

How do you understand the significance of baptism in relation to participation in the local church?

6. What do you think Jesus meant by this statement: "It is proper for us to do this to fulfill all righteousness"? (v. 15) Think through the many prophetic references of chapter 2 before you answer.

STUDY FOUR
Matthew 4

Measure of the King

A striking contrast greets us in Matthew 4. Matthew brings us crashing back to reality by emphasizing not only the presence but the determined devices of the devil. The righteousness of the Saviour calls forth once again the rebellion of the serpent. Like Jesus, those who live in obedience to the Heavenly Father stand in constant danger of attack by the evil one.

Many have pondered the meaning of temptation as it is described in the first part of chapter 4. The word (*parazo*) means to try, attempt, test, or endeavor. Here the context clearly suggests a test in the moral and spiritual realm. Satan attempts to entice the humanity of Christ, urging Him to go beyond moral boundaries set by God. It is helpful to remember that Jesus Himself was tempted, emphasizing that temptation itself is not a sin.

The Gospel of Matthew

A. MEASURE OF HIS CHARACTER (*Matt. 4:1-11*). Several crucial questions come to mind in this dramatic passage. Was the temptation of Christ real? When tempted, could Christ have actually sinned? What form did Satan take as he confronted Jesus in the desert? These questions are not easily answered, but they are worthy of our consideration as we think through these 11 verses.

Examining the Text

1. Read Matthew 4:1-11. Categorize the three temptations Satan put before the Lord in this passage.

2. Why was it necessary for Christ to be tempted? See Hebrews 2 and 1 Corinthians 10.

3. In these verses find and state several evidences of Jesus' purity and loyalty to the Father.

4. Four Old Testament texts are quoted by Jesus in this chapter. Look them up and read them in context:

Deuteronomy 8:3

Explaining the Text

1. Satan is known by many names in the Bible—adversary, Beelzebub, Belial, deceiver. Matthew's choice of *diabolos* emphasizes Satan's role as slanderer in this temptation narrative.

2. Most evangelicals argue that Christ could not have sinned because He was God as well as man. Nevertheless, the test and conflict were real even though the outcome was never in doubt.

Explaining the Text	*Examining the Text*
	Psalm 91:11-12
	Deuteronomy 6:16
	Deuteronomy 6:13

B. MEASURE OF HIS TRAVEL (*Matt. 4:12-17*). Geography is always important in the Scriptures, especially as we try to understand the ministry of Christ and the growth of the early church. In this passage, Matthew links the prophecies of Isaiah with the appearance of the Messiah and records His first public message.

Explaining the Text	*Examining the Text*
1. None of the Gospel writers is particularly intent on telling every aspect of Christ's story, but a harmony of the Gospels can help you follow the chronological flow of events.	1. Read Matthew 4:12-17. Locate each of the geographical references in these six verses in a Bible atlas.
2. The phrase "kingdom of heaven" appears at least 33 times in the Book of Matthew. It can be traced back to Daniel 2:44 and 7:13-14 where it is associated with Christ's coming messianic kingdom.	2. To what lake is Matthew referring in verse 13?
	3. Review Matthew 3:1-12. Compare John's message with that of Jesus. How are they alike? How are they different?

C. MEASURE OF HIS FOLLOWERS (*Matt. 4:18-22*). A contemporary Christian song reminds us that "God uses ordinary people." That is evident in our lives as it was in the lives of the early disciples. Four fishermen were called from simple daily tasks to divine service by the Master Himself.

Examining the Text

1. Read Matthew 4:18-22. Notice the instant obedience of these first disciples when Jesus called them. Write a few sentences showing how their behavior contrasted with common problems of Israel in the Old Testament.

2. Why did Jesus select these four men first? Was it just that they were handy in Capernaum? Did their occupation have anything to do with the choice? What other factors might have been involved?

Explaining the Text

1. Here the word *preparing* seems like a common term describing the everyday chores of a fisherman (v. 21). In Ephesians 4, Paul gives the same Greek word a theological dynamic when he states that gifted leaders in the church are "to prepare God's people for works of service" (4:12).

D. MEASURE OF HIS MINISTRY (*Matt. 4:23-25*). Three present tense verbs launch this paragraph—*teaching*, *preaching*, and *healing*. Matthew wants us to picture the early Galilean ministry of the Lord as He touched the lives of people physically and spiritually.

Measure of the King

Explaining the Text	*Examining the Text*
1. Though not as important as His message, Jesus' miracles authenticated His messiahship.	1. Read Matthew 4:23-25. Find Syria on a map of the first century and then on a map of the 20th century. Compare the areas involved.
	2. What do you think Jesus might have said when "preaching the good news of the kingdom"? (v. 23)

Experiencing the Text

1. Jesus fasted "forty days and forty nights." Take a look at Exodus 24:18 and 1 Kings 19:8. How can fasting be a spiritual exercise for Christians today?

2. How does Christ's coping with temptation in the wilderness set an example for us today?

3. Remember your study of repentance in lesson 3? Is Jesus calling for something different than John now that the Messiah has already come?

4. Define discipleship. How can we make disciples today?

5. Which of the temptations that Jesus overcame is most like temptations that trouble you?

6. How can you apply the scriptural principles that Jesus drew on to overcome your own temptations?

7. In one sentence, write the central spiritual lesson of this passage (vv. 1-11).

STUDY FIVE
Matthew 5

Message of the King—Part 1

The Sermon on the Mount is one of the best-known portions of the Bible—and one of the most misunderstood. Several guidelines help us in our interpretation of this passage. First of all, the sermon was clearly given to Jews and to followers who at least professed to be disciples. Like the focus of most of Matthew, these verses center on the kingdom.

Essentially the nature of the Sermon on the Mount is ethical teaching which serves as a counterpart to the Old Testament Law. Jesus wants to correct a false Jewish concentration on the material aspects of the kingdom and try to show His followers that the primary focus aims at the hearts of people.

True, Christ's literal kingdom is yet to come, but today's Christian is a part of the kingdom because he belongs to the family of the King. Therefore, the principles of the Sermon on the Mount apply to us as believers, especially since much of this teaching is repeated in various forms throughout the epistles.

A. CHARACTERISTICS OF KINGDOM CITIZENS (*Matt. 5:1-12*). The term *beatitudes* comes from the Latin word meaning *blessed* or *happy*. Essentially it describes an inner condition which might also be called "spiritual prosperity." These verses remind us of the unconditional blessing of the righteous person described in Psalm 1.

Examining the Text	*Explaining the Text*
1. Read Matthew 5:1-12. How do you reconcile a statement like, "Blessed are those who mourn"? (v. 4) What kind of mourning in the life of a Christian can possibly lead to happiness?	1. First century Jews thought material prosperity was a sign of God's favor. In these verses, Jesus shows that helpless people turn to God and, therefore, receive spiritual prosperity.
2. What do you think it means to "hunger and thirst for righteousness"? (v. 6)	2. Here the Lord contrasts the one who waits for God's grace and the one who tries to take the world by his own force.
3. What are some practical applications of the concept of peacemaking in today's world?	3. Mercy is a reflection of one of God's central attributes and stands in contrast with rigid judgment.
4. To whom are these beatitudes spoken? Study verses 1-2 carefully before you answer.	

Message of the King 39

B. FUNCTIONS OF KINGDOM CITIZENS (*Matt. 5:13-16*). Metaphors are common in the Bible. For example, the church is described as the body of Christ, a family, a building, a nation, and numerous other ways. In these important verses, the followers of the Lord are called salt and light, two metaphors which are as relevant today as they were when spoken almost 2,000 years ago.

Explaining the Text	*Examining the Text*
1. The Holy Spirit in believers provides a presence in the world which keeps the whole pagan pottage from rotting completely. The history of the church demonstrates this "salting" influence of the Gospel.	1. Read Matthew 5:13-16. In addition to preservation, name several other qualities or uses of salt. How can these be applied to Christian living? 2. In what ways can Christians be viewed as "cities on a hill"? (v. 14) 3. The doing of good deeds has an ultimate motive. Can you find and write it?

C. STANDARDS OF KINGDOM CITIZENS (*Matt. 5:17-48*). This is a long section, but in order to be true to the flow of the text we need to see it as a complete section in itself. Essentially it deals with Christ and the Law. Before setting kingdom standards, Christ deals with how people under grace relate to law in general and the Ten Commandments more directly. He emphasizes that He didn't come to set aside the Law but to fulfill it. Notice that the Lord is not talking about how to be saved but rather how saved people display righteousness in their lives.

Examining the Text	*Explaining the Text*
1. Read Matthew 5:17-48. Verses 23 and 24 lay down a very interesting pattern for correcting minor grievances before they get too serious. Name some specific ways these verses could be applied in your family. In your church. On your job.	
2. What did the Lord mean when He said, "It is better for you to lose one part of your body than for your whole body to go into hell"? (v. 30)	
3. Sound, Bible-believing Christians disagree widely about the issue of divorce, but the Holy Spirit can give you an understanding of what He wants you to believe. List one or two things you believe this passage teaches about divorce.	3. In this passage, the emphasis of the Lord is more on the wicked heart than the overt act of adultery.
4. Think of some examples of vows or covenants we make in today's society. How has society encouraged us to break them?	4. Vows and oaths were a great part of Jewish life, but their sacredness had greatly deteriorated by the time of Christ. The Lord points out that kingdom citizens should be so devoted to truth that everything they say will be fact.

Message of the King

Explaining the Text

5. First-century Jews tended to love their friends and hate their enemies, but Jesus taught that loving one's enemies reflects the attitude of God Himself, who sent His Son to die for those who hated Him.

Examining the Text

5. What do you think Jesus meant when He said, "Be perfect, therefore, as your heavenly Father is perfect"? (v. 48)

Experiencing the Text

1. Rewrite the eight beatitudes in your own words.

2. Name some ways Christians suffer persecution today specifically because of Christ.

3. In what ways can we assure that God's glory really motivates our behavior?

4. Name some practical applications of the Ten Commandments today.

5. Some Christians believe that the Sermon on the Mount (vv. 33-37) prohibits taking oaths in a court of law. How do you respond to that interpretation?

STUDY SIX

Matthew 6

Message of the King—Part 2

Worldliness is any attitude which takes our focus away from the spiritual kingdom and places it on the present earthly kingdom temporarily run by what Jesus called "the kings of the Gentiles." The Sermon on the Mount offers an antidote to worldly thinking. It calls on the disciples of Jesus to live "otherworldly" lifestyles in relation to social needs, personal spiritual life, ownership of things, and worry. What a practical chapter in a day in which stress and pressure represent major health hazards in Western society.

In our last study we reviewed the characteristics, functions and standards of kingdom citizens. Now our Lord teaches us about the attitudes of those citizens toward common but important issues of life.

A. ATTITUDE TOWARD GIVING (*Matt. 6:1-4*). The Pharisees had set the tone for public religion, but now Jesus called His disciples to a different kind of worship. Righteous giving is not to be done for the praise of men, but so that the Heavenly Father who sees everything done in secret can reward the truly generous giver.

Examining the Text	*Explaining the Text*
1. Read Matthew 6:1-4. According to the passage, why should Christ's disciples avoid ostentatious giving?	1. The issue here is motive and the words *to be seen* translate a Greek word from which we get the English word *theatric*. The Christian's giving is not to be an act performed for an audience.
2. What does Jesus describe as the real motive of the hypocrites when they gave money for the needy?	2. Jesus may have been referring to a trumpet-shaped metal chest in which coins would make a clanging sound when heavily dropped.
3. Rephrase in your own words the command, "Do not let your left hand know what your right hand is doing" (v. 3).	

B. ATTITUDE TOWARD PRAYER AND FASTING (*Matt. 6:5-18*). Jews were to pray at certain hours of the day. It would have been easy for the Pharisees to pray at highly visible locations during those hours so that as many as possible could watch them in their faithful adherence to the laws of prayer. The same attitude applied to fasting—hypocrites arranged to look gaunt and hungry to demonstrate their overt righteousness. But Jesus calls for private righteousness seen and rewarded only by the Father. Obviously the Father values sincerity of heart over the repetition of endless words.

Explaining the Text	Examining the Text
	1. Read Matthew 6:5-18. Verses 9-13 are commonly called the "Lord's Prayer." Is this a good title? Why or why not?
2. Note that the content of this model prayer aims first at God, then at our needs. Some have called it a kingdom prayer or a family prayer which provides a pattern for a God-centered spirit of praying.	2. Thinking in terms of modern society, how do you understand the phrase, "Your will be done on earth as it is in heaven"? (v. 10)
	3. How do you interpret Jesus' words, "Put oil on your head and wash your face"? (v. 17)
	4. Why does the Bible teach fasting "in secret"?

C. ATTITUDE TOWARD WEALTH (*Matt. 6:19-24*). First-century Jews equated material wealth with blessing from God, but Jesus rebuked them for such worldly thinking. When covetous eyes focus on money, one's whole life is dark. On the other hand, when one chooses to be God's servant, his life is characterized by light and love.

Examining the Text	*Explaining the Text*
1. Read Matthew 6:19-24. Name some specific kinds of "treasures" subject to loss by moth, rust, or thieves.	
2. How do you understand the phrase, "If your eyes are bad, your whole body will be full of darkness"? (v. 23)	2. The eyes obviously serve as the focus of the body since through them covetousness can come.
3. In what other ways might the guideline in verse 24 be applied?	

D. ATTITUDE TOWARD WORRY (*Matt. 6:25-34*). There is an obvious link between concern for earthly treasure and the anxiety that comes when you have (or desire) it. Jesus compares God's concern for His children to His care of nature, urging His followers to forsake worry.

Examining the Text	*Explaining the Text*
1. Read Matthew 6:25-34. About what specific things does this passage teach Christians not to worry?	

Message of the King 47

Explaining the Text

2. Notice how one's attitudes toward giving, prayer, and material possessions lead up to a kingdom mentality of leaving things to the care of the Heavenly Father.

3. Seeking the kingdom is a reference to following the values and lifestyle described by Jesus throughout the Sermon on the Mount.

Examining the Text

2. List all the reasons for not worrying mentioned in this passage.

3. Explain the phrase, "Tomorrow will worry about itself" (v. 34).

Experiencing the Text

1. How can you make sure your giving is done in "secret"?

2. How does this chapter apply to the teaching of pledges and faith promises?

3. Rewrite the Lord's Prayer in your own words, giving it a contemporary flavor.

4. Should verses 14-15 be taken literally? Will God's forgiveness be withheld if we fail to forgive others?

5. Identify some specific ways you can "store up treasures in heaven."

6. What are some ways that Christians serve money today?

7. Give some examples of God's care in nature.

8. Review Matthew 6:33. Memorize this helpful Scripture if you have never done so.

9. Name some values of fasting as a spiritual exercise for today.

STUDY SEVEN
Matthew 7

Message of the King—Part 3

Leo Tolstoy once wrote, "One can live magnificently in this world if one knows how to work and how to love, to work for the person one loves, and to love one's work." One might paraphrase that dramatic sentence in light of the present day church: "One can lead competently in God's church, if one knows how to serve and how to love; to serve the persons one loves and to love one's service."

The seventh chapter of Matthew reveals the responsibilities of kingdom citizens. In the first part of the chapter, those responsibilities are directed toward others as the Lord rebukes harsh judgment, suggests careful discrimination in our reactions and attitudes toward others, and tells us that the wisdom for right reactions will be given us through prayer.

In the second part of the chapter (vv. 13-29), the emphasis seems to be on the responsibilities of kingdom citizens toward themselves. The disciples received admonition to walk the narrow way, avoid false teachers, and build their lives solidly on the rock of obedience to Christ.

These are the principles of kingdom life, binding upon all who consider themselves a part of the King's family. The Lord compares five aspects of kingdom living, showing His subjects how to reject the false and adopt the true.

A. TRUE AND FALSE JUDGMENT (*Matt. 7:1-6*). When we properly ignore the chapter break, we see that Jesus moves immediately from the problem of worry to the problem of judging others. The issue is not that judgment should never occur, but that only those who have first accurately judged themselves and allowed God to take care of the problems in their lives are in a position to judge others. A wise Christian helps others when he sees that his assistance has reasonable opportunity of being accepted and utilized.

Examining the Text

1. Read Matthew 7:1-6. Why did the Lord offer such a strong warning against judging other people, and, in particular, why does it appear in the Sermon on the Mount?

2. Whom does Jesus address as a hypocrite in verse 5? The entire crowd on the mountain? The disciples? The Pharisees and religious leaders?

3. Whom do you think Jesus had in mind when He spoke of "dogs" and "pigs"?

Explaining the Text

1. The word *judgment*, from which we get our English word *crisis*, describes a decision between two values which involves the weighing of evidence in the passing of a sentence.

3. Since they considered dogs and pigs unclean, within the context of this brief parable, the Jews would be incapable of grasping the value of pearls.

B. TRUE AND FALSE PRAYING *(Matt. 7:7-12)*. This significant section on prayer appears in similar form in Luke 11, offering a study in action/reaction and comparison/contrast. When the Lord's disciples ask, seek, and knock, they receive, find, and see the door opened. Although the Heavenly Father can be compared with an earthly father in the sense that both want the best for their children, the love of the Heavenly Father is infinitely greater and serves as a major impetus to prayer.

Explaining the Text	*Examining the Text*
1. Because all three verbs are present imperatives, Jesus is really commanding His followers to keep on asking, keep on seeking, and keep on knocking.	1. Read Matthew 7:7-12. How do the three words—ask, seek, and knock—differ when describing prayer activity?
	2. What kinds of good gifts does the Heavenly Father give? What kinds of good gifts do we need from Him?
	3. How does verse 12 fit in this section on prayer? Doesn't the theme of prayer seem to end at verse 11? How do you explain the tacking on of the Golden Rule at this point?

The Gospel of Matthew

C. TRUE AND FALSE GOSPEL (*Matt. 7:13-14*). Despite what many religious teachers proclaim, the path to the kingdom is narrow, and few find it. The people of God have always been a small remnant, in the Old Testament and at the present hour.

Examining the Text	*Explaining the Text*
1. Read Matthew 7:13-14. Find and compare five adjectives or adverbs in these two verses. Why did the Lord use so many, and what do they signify?	1. These two verses expose the false teaching that a gracious and loving God will eventually find a way to save everybody, whether or not they know of or trust Christ's death on the cross.
2. Why do only a few find the narrow road that leads to life?	

D. TRUE AND FALSE TEACHERS (*Matt. 7:15-23*). The mid-1980s offered an epidemic of government leaks, trading of spy secrets, and revealing of security secrets. In almost every case, the danger has been from within the government organizations themselves. That's what these eight verses tell us about the Lord's people—the major danger lies not with atheists and secular humanists, but with those who pretend to be true religious teachers.

Examining the Text	*Explaining the Text*
1. Read Matthew 7:15-23. These verses contain a number of metaphors which we need to identify. For example, "fruit" stands for behavior or actions. Try giving a meaning to the rest of the metaphors:	1. This passage shows that actions, not words, reflect the truth or error of one's teaching.

Explaining the Text	Examining the Text
	Sheep's clothing
	Ferocious wolves
	Good tree
	Bad tree
	Good fruit
	Bad fruit
	2. The evildoers who are turned away seem surprised since they have proclaimed the Lord's name. What did these evildoers lack that caused them to be barred from the kingdom?

E. TRUE AND FALSE FOUNDATIONS (*Matt. 7:24-29*). The word for *rock* is *petra*, a rock ledge that commonly served as the foundation for a house or a cliff (Matt. 16:18). Jesus commonly divides people into two groups—saved and unsaved, narrow way and broad way, sheep and goats, and here, sand builders and rock builders.

Examining the Text

1. Read Matthew 7:24-29. Using a good concordance, locate several other New Testament passages where Christ is referred to as a rock.

2. Apart from where they chose to build, what other differences does this passage attribute to these two builders?

3. Why did this difference in teaching style amaze the people so much? Why did the teachers of the Law fail to teach with authority?

Explaining the Text

2. Notice that these builders seem to have used the same materials and their finished products seem to have been put to the same test.

3. The teachers of the Law regularly taught using multiple quotations from rabbinical literature to substantiate their claims.

Experiencing the Text

1. How can we avoid being judgmental hypocrites?

2. Name some specific things to keep in mind when approaching "speck-eyed" people.

3. How can we know when not to share the Gospel, in order to avoid throwing pearls to pigs?

4. Can verses 7-8 be considered an absolute prayer promise? What other biblical factors must be taken into consideration?

5. Respond to the statement, "When evangelical Christians get to heaven, they're going to see many more people there than they ever expected."

6. Write a brief synopsis of the warnings of this chapter.

7. Write a brief paragraph about your own prayer life.

8. Using just one word each, characterize the wise builder and the foolish builder.

9. List some ways your life will change because you have studied the Sermon on the Mount.

STUDY EIGHT

Matthew 8–9

Miracles of the King

Miracle—what an interesting modern-day word! If an usually disobedient child goes to bed without complaining, his mother might exclaim, "It's a miracle—he's never done that before." Or a college student failing to study for a test yet winding up with a B might announce, "It's a miracle." Like many other Bible words, we have diluted "miracle" until it means nothing more than a somewhat unusual occurrence.

Not so in these chapters before us. Matthew records approximately 21 miracles in his book, and 10 of them appear in chapters 8 and 9. A simple but adequate definition for our purposes might look like this: "A miracle is the introduction of a supernatural element into the natural order." Bible miracles sometimes take the form of wonders, signs, power, or special works of God.

The miracles of the Lord seem to have special characteristics. First of all, He performs them with ease. Secondly, there is never an outside person involved, only the Son of God Himself. Finally, His miracles are performed almost exclusively in the sphere of human life, evidencing the great grace and mercy of the Lord.

A. MIRACLES IN CAPERNAUM (*Matt. 8:1-22*). The arrangement of these two chapters is difficult since our overview will not permit a miracle-by-miracle analysis. Instead we'll follow Jesus geographically from Capernaum across the lake to Gadara, back to Capernaum, and then on a tour throughout Galilee. In this first section, three miracles unfold—the healing of the leper, the healing of the palsied servant, and the healing of Peter's mother-in-law. These are followed by a dramatic parenthesis in which the Lord issues a strategic call for disciples.

Examining the Text	*Explaining the Text*
1. Read Matthew 8:1-22. What did the leper have to do in order to be made clean?	1. Leprosy is almost always a type of sin, reminding Bible readers of the physical/spiritual curse of the Fall.
2. What astonished Jesus in the incident with the centurion—the faith of the Gentile or the extent of Jewish unbelief?	2. Only an unusual Roman officer would have been concerned for his slaves.
3. Review Isaiah 53:4 and suggest why Matthew includes that Old Testament quotation in verse 17.	3. Notice in every case there is an instantaneous healing and return to health, not a slow period of convalescence.
4. In view of the Bible's strong emphasis on families, why would Jesus say what He did in verse 22?	

Miracles of the King 59

B. MIRACLES AMONG THE GADARENES (*Matt. 8:23-34*). In showing Jesus' humanity, Matthew once again tells us He was asleep in the boat during the storm. The focus of this Scripture is not the sin of the disciples, nor the reality of demons, but the sovereignty of the Son of God over nature.

Explaining the Text	*Examining the Text*
1. In the incident on the lake, the disciples' failure seems to be their excessive terror, not their seeking help from the Lord.	1. Read Matthew 8:23-34. Apart from physical safety, what spiritual or discipling purposes might the Lord have intended in calming the storm?
2. Josephus, in his *Antiquities of the Jews*, suggests that these pigs may have been Jewish herds and, therefore, in violation of Mosaic Law, accounting for the Lord's allowing them to drown.	2. Why did the demons beg to go into the herd of pigs?
	3. How do you account for the response of the Gadarenes when "they pleaded with Him to leave their region"? (v. 34)

C. MIRACLES BACK IN CAPERNAUM (*Matt. 9:1-26*). Though Jesus was born in Bethlehem and raised in Nazareth, Capernaum is sometimes considered to be Jesus' home city (v. 1). Here, Jesus healed the paralytic, called Matthew to discipleship, answered questions about fasting, and performed one of three resurrections recorded during His ministry.

Examining the Text

1. Read Matthew 9:1-26. How do you account for the difference in the crowd's attitude between verses 3 and 8?

2. What did Jesus want His followers to learn about mercy and sacrifice in verse 13?

3. The synopsis indicates Jesus took part in three resurrections. In addition to Jairus' daughter, can you remember the other two? If you have any trouble, check out John 11 and Luke 7.

4. Look again at verse 20. What can you tell from that verse about the woman's concept of healing?

Explaining the Text

1. Notice that Jesus commends the faith of the people who brought the paralytic.

Miracles of the King

D. MIRACLES THROUGHOUT GALILEE (*Matt. 9:27-38*).

Specific accounts of the healing of two blind men and a demoniac lead Matthew to describe the big picture: "Jesus went through all the towns and villages, teaching in their synagogues, preaching the good news of the kingdom, and healing every disease and sickness" (v. 35). No longer confined to a few select cities, Jesus' ministry now branched out all over northern Israel.

Explaining the Text	*Examining the Text*
1. This account is found only in Matthew and emphasizes the faith of those who were healed.	1. Read Matthew 9:27-38. Since Jesus warned the blind men not to report the miracle, do you find flagrant disobedience in their behavior? If so, why were they not punished?
	2. Why did the Pharisees attribute Jesus' miracle-working power to demon possession? (v. 34)
3. Matthew wants us to know that Jesus taught and preached as He shepherded the helpless sheep of Israel.	3. Whom did Jesus have in mind as "the Lord of the Harvest"? (v. 38)

Experiencing the Text

1. Faith dominates these two chapters. When did you exercise the greatest faith in God? What were the results?

2. The discipleship command in 8:22 seems harsh. How does this command relate to your responsibility to follow Jesus today?

3. Using a Bible dictionary, research the origin of demons, and what is meant by "the appointed time" in 8:29.

4. How would you answer someone who argued that Jesus practiced cruelty to animals by allowing the herd of pigs to drown in the lake?

5. The paralytic's life was dramatically changed the day he met Jesus. How has your life changed since trusting Jesus Christ?

6. Restate the Parable of the Wine and Wineskins in contemporary terminology related to your life.

7. What lessons can you learn from the behavior of the synagogue ruler? (9:18-26) Think particularly about his emotions when Jesus stopped to speak to the woman who was hemorrhaging.

8. Consider some implications of praying for workers for the harvest. What is your responsibility in this need?

STUDY NINE
Matthew 10

Men of the King

Jesus' mission was now in full swing, but he needed to pull together His missionary team. These 12 messengers (or at least 11 of them) became the core leadership of the New Testament church. Selected by the Lord Himself, they were given distinctive purposes, positions, and performance expectations.

Larry Burkett, founder of Christian Financial Concepts, described his call to ministry by referring to the lives of the disciples. In the true style of a businessman, he listed in two columns the positive and negative traits of these men at the time of their selection. On completing the project, he discovered he had an entire page of negative traits and only a few positive traits. Skeptical before the exercise, Burkett then concluded that if God could use these 12 men, He could use Burkett as well.

Encouragement rests in the record of the disciples, their achievements, and their failures. They were ordinary men chosen for an extraordinary task. The chapter before us in this study describes the selection of the Twelve, their ministry, and their relationship to Christ. As modern-day disciples, we can find helpful lessons strewn throughout the chapter like flakes of gold in a prospector's stream.

A. MESSENGERS FOR THE MISSION (*Matt. 10:1-4*). Though the actual selecting of the Twelve is recorded in Mark 3:13-19 and Luke 6:12-16, here we have Matthew's list with its emphasis on authority. It is fitting to find this first New Testament list of disciples immediately following Jesus' command to pray to the Father for workers (9:38).

Examining the Text	*Explaining the Text*
1. Read Matthew 10:1-4. Compare this list of disciples with the lists found in Mark and Luke. How are they alike or different?	1. The word *disciple* means learner or student, while the word *apostle* refers to a delegator or messenger sent with orders. The word *apostle* is used 79 times in the New Testament.
2. As you study the lists of disciples, notice who heads up all four lists. Who is last in each list? How do the first four names differ in each list?	
3. Why did Jesus choose 12 disciples rather than some other number?	

B. METHODOLOGY FOR THE MISSION (*Matt. 10:5-15*). Whenever the church undertakes a mission there are logistical problems, as described by this portion of the chapter. Jesus first taught the disciples about their destination. Then he explained their declaration, emphasized the importance of determination, and reminded them that those who refuse will incur damnation.

Men of the King

Explaining the Text	*Examining the Text*
1. Remember the Gospel was very restricted in its offer at this time. The message of the disciples centered on the kingdom offer to Israel.	1. Read Matthew 10:5-15. In light of the entire New Testament, why were these disciples sent only to "the lost sheep of Israel"? (v. 6)
2. Different aspects of this mission refer to different time periods in the lives of the disciples. This section covers the time from their call to the crucifixion.	2. Make a list of the specific things the messengers were to do. How does this list compare with the ministry of today's church?
3. The word *preach* means to herald or proclaim. It is often used to describe the announcing of results at athletic games or to identify a spokesman for a king.	3. In verses 9-10, note the things the disciples were not to take. Why was their equipment so scanty? Consider verses 11-15 in your answer.

C. MYSTERIES OF THE MISSION (*Matt. 10:16-23*). Every serious mission for the Lord carries some danger and frustration with events and issues we may not understand. In these verses, Jesus broadened the picture with his inclusion of apostolic persecution after the Resurrection.

Examining the Text

1. Read Matthew 10:16-23. Can you name specific instances when the Lord's disciples (apostles) were handed over to councils and flogged? See Acts 5:40-42; 7:54-60; 12:1-4.

2. Name some time in the New Testament when the Lord's people witnessed to governors and kings.

3. What do you think the Lord meant by "He who stands firm to the end will be saved"? (v. 22)

Explaining the Text

1. The phrase "sheep among wolves" points to the innocence of believers in a cruel world (v. 16).

3. The reference in verse 20 is the first mention of the Holy Spirit in the Book of Matthew.

D. MASTER OF THE MISSION (*Matt. 10:24-33*). All disciples need to learn obedience to the Lord, and this section teaches us about the Master of the mission. The disciples developed important relationships with the Master. They carefully learned revelations from Him and began to exercise proper response. Even though some of these things may have specific fulfillments which are yet future, the general principles still relate to us today.

Men of the King

Explaining the Text	Examining the Text
1. Beelzebub is a reference to Satan himself (v. 25). Since Jesus was called Satan, His followers should expect the same treatment.	1. Read Matthew 10:24-33. Name several ways the messengers on this mission were to be like their Master.
2. Certainly Satan was not in the Lord's mind when He talked about the One who can destroy both soul and body in hell; Christians are never told to fear Satan.	2. Of whom were Jesus' disciples to be afraid?
	3. In light of your understanding of the doctrine of salvation, how do you interpret verse 33?

E. MOTIVES FOR THE MISSION (*Matt. 10:34-42*). The Bible always forces us to consider our motivation. Why do we witness for Christ? Why do we teach Sunday School? Why do we send out missionaries? The final portion of this chapter deals with motives for missionary spirit, motives for missionary service, and motives for missionary support.

Explaining the Text	Examining the Text
1. Notice how the Gospel does not always bring world peace, family unity, and brotherly love.	1. Read Matthew 10:34-42. Study Micah 7:6-7 and explain in simple terms how the Gospel can divide a family as verses 35-36 suggest.

Examining the Text

2. Why is it wrong to put one's family ahead of one's love for Christ?

3. What does it mean to "receive a prophet because he is a prophet" or "receive a righteous man because he is a righteous man"? (v. 41) How is that different from the kind of motivation described in verse 42?

Explaining the Text

2. Verse 38 provides us with the first mention of the Cross in the New Testament.

3. The word *receives* appears eight times in verses 40-41, describing the attitude the Lord's people ought to have toward His servants.

Experiencing the Text

1. List at least three ways in which you believe you are a disciple (apostle) of the Lord?

2. In what ways can you be like the people described as "worthy" in verses 11-13?

3. How does Jesus' missionary strategy relate to our missions organizations today?

4. Describe specific ways in which Christians can be "shrewd as snakes and innocent as doves" (v. 16).

5. Can you think of any time or way in which you were persecuted for serving the Lord? How did you respond? What did you learn from that experience?

6. Reread Matthew 10:30. In what ways have you experienced God's care?

7. In the application of this passage, we could say there are messages for proud Christians, frightened Christians, and non-Christians. Find and write them in simple terms.

8. Name some ways that Christians can give a "cup of cold water to one of these little ones" (v. 42).

STUDY TEN
Matthew 11–12

Magnitude of the King

These chapters represent the inauguration of Christ's great preaching ministry in Galilee. The record is not necessarily chronological, nor the events specifically related to one another; but all show in some way the grandeur and magnificence of the Messiah. We also see that opposition to the kingdom Gospel is rapidly growing.

As we noted in the last study, the Twelve were sent on a mission. Now Jesus departs alone to teach and preach throughout the cities of Galilee. Spread before us in these two chapters is the isolation of pure righteousness in the person of Christ, standing against the wickedness and darkness of the world all around Him.

A. JESUS AND JOHN (*Matt. 11:1-15*). The first part of our study shows the magnitude of the Messiah in relation to the forerunner. It is not strange that John's faith began to waver since he was the divinely ordained prophet sent ahead of the Messiah. The Messiah was supposed to correct the abuses of the world, but John saw very little evidence of renewal at this point. The Lord's pictorial answer to John authenticates the prophet's expectation of a literal kingdom.

Examining the Text	*Explaining the Text*
1. Read Matthew 11:1-15. Jesus offered several answers to John's question in verse 3. List them here.	1. In verse 3, the phrase "the one who was to come" (*hoerchomenos*) is a title for the Messiah.
2. Why do you think Jesus waited till John's disciples had left before praising the prophet in such glowing terms?	2. The prophetic ministries of both John and Jesus regularly review Old Testament passages like the quotation in verse 10 from Malachi 3:1.
3. What did Jesus mean when He said, "He who is least in the kingdom of heaven is greater than he"? (v. 11)	

Magnitude of the King   73

B. JESUS AND UNBELIEVERS (*Matt. 11:16-24*). John came with a serious message of repentance. Christ came with a joyous Gospel offering rest and peace. Yet neither had an effect on the hardness of unbelieving hearts. Because they had opportunity to hear both John and Jesus, cities of the first century came under greater condemnation than the ancient cities who knew only the limited message of Jehovah available in that day.

Explaining the Text	*Examining the Text*
	1. Read Matthew 11:16-24. Explain Jesus' use of the parable in verse 17.
2. These three cities—Korazin, Bethsaida, and Capernaum—exemplify the attitude of a rejecting nation. Verse 21 offers the first "woe" in a long series of such condemnations found throughout Matthew's Gospel.	2. Verses 22 and 24 seem to suggest degrees of punishment. What implications might we draw from that, with respect to Christ-rejectors in our day?

C. JESUS AND BELIEVERS (*Matt. 11:25-30; 12:46-50*). We take these two sections together because, though they appear in different chapters, they are spoken to the same group of people. Childlike faith marks the disciples of the Lord and unlocks for them the key of understanding to His revelation. They are closer to Him than members of His own earthly family, and He gives to them rest and deliverance from the burdens of this world.

Explaining the Text	*Examining the Text*
	1. Who are those to whom the Son chooses to reveal Himself?

The Gospel of Matthew

Examining the Text	*Explaining the Text*
2. Read Matthew 11:25-30 and 12:46-50. When Jesus spoke of "little children" He was probably referring to the disciples. Whom might Jesus have been referring to when He spoke of the "wise and learned"? (v. 25)	2. Salvation comes not by wisdom, scientific proof, or irrefutable logic. It comes rather in simple faith given as a gift from the Heavenly Father.
3. In these passages, Jesus describes Himself intimately. List everything He tells us about Himself.	3. The phrase "Take my yoke" referred to a rabbinical student submitting himself to his teacher.

D. JESUS AND THE SABBATH (*Matt. 12:1-21*). These verses establish the dominance of the person of Christ over religious legalism. The Son of God is more important than any given day or place. Remember the concept of the Sabbath (seventh day) is purely a Jewish practice having no validity in New Testament Christianity.

Examining the Text	*Explaining the Text*
1. Read Matthew 12:1-21. Jesus refuted the Pharisees' legalism by referring to the three portions of the Old Testament—the Historical books, the Law, and the Prophets. Read 1 Samuel 21:1-6, Numbers 28: 9-10, and Hosea 6:6 to get a better picture of what Jesus was saying. Then read Colossians 2:14-17 for a New Testament perspective on the legalism of special days.	1. Since the Pharisees seemed to attach no stigma to David's act or that of the priests, we may conclude that their position rested on some new Talmudic additions to the Law, probably written 100–200 years before the birth of Christ.

Magnitude of the King 75

Explaining the Text	*Examining the Text*
	2. How did the Pharisees respond to Jesus' logic? What important dimension of Jesus' ministry began to take form here?
3. References to the "bruised reed" and "smoldering wick" indicate the gentleness and kindness of Jesus.	3. Compare verses 14 and 21 to Isaiah 42:1-4. What events do you think this comparison suggests?

E. JESUS AND THE WICKED CIVILIZATION (*Matt. 12:22-45*). This passage describes one of the busiest days in Jesus' ministry. In every sense, the events are a confrontation of good and evil, righteousness and wickedness. It began with the presentation of a genuine hardship case—a demon-possessed man who was born blind and mute. This sparked a discussion about demons which continued through verse 45.

Explaining the Text	*Examining the Text*
1. Notice the two different reactions to the healing. The crowd concluded Jesus must be the Son of David, but the Pharisees, whose hearts were already hardened, saw it as the work of Satan.	1. Remember our Kingdom theme. Look carefully at verses 22-28. What do they teach us about the King?

Examining the Text

2. Read Matthew 12:22-45. Jesus first answered the Pharisees with simple logic. How does verse 29 fit into His argument?

3. What does it mean to speak a word against the Holy Spirit? See Mark 3:30.

4. How do you understand verse 36 in the light of the paragraph in which it appears?

5. Review the Parable of the Cast-out Demon in verses 43-45. Write in one sentence what this passage means today.

Explaining the Text

2. Blasphemy against the Holy Spirit, the so-called "unpardonable sin," is defined here as attributing to Satan what is really accomplished by the power of God.

Experiencing the Text

1. Have you ever had doubts as John did about Jesus? How were they finally solved?

Magnitude of the King 77

2. If someone were describing your ministry the way Jesus described John's, what might that person say?

3. If God's judgment was greater on first-century cities than on the ancient cities of the Old Testament, what implications might that have for countries who have had such easy access to the Gospel during the 20th century?

4. Review 11:25-30 and 12:46-50. Name some burdens you need to give to the Lord today.

5. Even though Sunday, the first day of the week, the day on which Christians worship (probably because of the Resurrection) is not the Sabbath, in what ways do you practice a day of rest in keeping with the general principle of the Sabbath?

6. Matthew 12:22-45 contains a lengthy section on demons and demonism. List three or four things you have learned about demons.

STUDY ELEVEN
Matthew 13:1-52

Mystery Reign of the King

Several strikingly important teachings confront us in this chapter, and all are essential to its understanding. First, we must notice the abundant use of simile and metaphor parables (seven in all). Second, the careful explanation of the parabolic method which appears here in detail is found nowhere else in the New Testament. Third, the uses of the word *kingdom* are important. In fact, the phrase "the kingdom of heaven is like" appears at least six times in this chapter. Finally, it's important to note that the explanation of several of the parables is offered only to the disciples.

The mystery reign of the King described in Matthew 13 explains Jesus' spiritual control over the earth during the time He is physically absent from us. This mystery reign is described or taught in parables which form the structure of our study.

A. PARABLE OF THE SOWER (*Matt. 13:1-23*). The sower is identified in Christ's interpretation of the second parable—"the one who sowed the good seed is the Son of Man" (v. 37). The four kinds of ground represent different human hearts. Notice only 25 percent of the hearers became fruitful, signifying that profession of religion rather than acceptance of the Gospel is commonplace during this mystery reign of the kingdom.

Examining the Text	*Explaining the Text*
1. Read Matthew 13:1-23. Make a three-column chart. In the first column, list the four kinds of ground. In the middle column, list the results of the seed. In the right column, write the reason for the results. Ground Seed Results	1. Notice that this teaching occurred on the same day that our Lord encountered and dealt with the tremendous opposition of chapter 12.
2. Add a fourth column to your chart, changing the soil metaphor to human hearts and showing what happens to the seed (the Word).	
3. In chapter 13, Jesus explained why He used parables. Rewrite that section in your own words.	3. Isaiah 6:9-10 explains the misunderstanding and rejection of the kingdom message. This Old Testament prophecy is used five times in the New Testament, always in connection with rejection.

B. PARABLE OF THE WEEDS (*Matt. 13:24-30, 36-43*). In this second parable, the "seed" represents believers rather than the Word. The parable describes mixed growth in the kingdom because Satan counterfeits genuine children of the King. Sowing time is apparently this present age, and the harvest will come at the judgment when the true nature of all people will be revealed.

Explaining the Text	*Examining the Text*
1. The word *weeds* means a plant which resembles wheat but whose grains are black. Only when the black grain forms can the plants be separated.	1. Read Matthew 13:24-30, 36-43. Identify all the metaphors of this parable: sower enemy wheat weeds servants harvesters 2. How does the Parable of the Weeds relate to us today?

C. PARABLES OF THE MUSTARD SEED AND YEAST (*Matt. 13:31-35*). The abnormal growth of the mystery form of the kingdom comes into view here since the mustard plant is at best a shrub. Some have suggested that reference to birds is taken from Daniel 4 and meant to imply evil. Following the one-verse record of the Parable of Yeast, Jesus again explains why He uses parabolic teaching.

Examining the Text	*Explaining the Text*
1. Read Matthew 13:31-35. Briefly explain the Parable of the Mustard Seed.	1. Actually the mustard seed is not the smallest seed we know about today, but we must understand that designation in the light of seeds planted in the first century.
2. If the yeast is something evil, what does it represent in this parable?	
3. Jesus quotes Psalm 78:2 to explain why He used parables so frequently. What does this passage tell us about that Psalm?	

D. PARABLES OF THE TREASURE AND THE PEARL (*Matt. 13:44-46*). These closely linked parables both reflect divine viewpoint rather than human viewpoint. The key to both parables is identifying the central words: *treasure* and *pearl.*

Many and varied interpretations have been offered. One thing should be emphasized: salvation is not for sale and, even if it were, we have nothing to offer God in order to purchase it.

Explaining the Text	*Examining the Text*
	1. Read Matthew 13:44-46. Assuming the treasure might refer to Israel, how do the two parts of the parable come together? 2. Assume for a moment that the pearl refers to salvation. How would you rewrite the parable using salvation as the centerpiece?

E. PARABLE OF THE NET (*Matt. 13:47-52*). These verses contain a similar message to that of the previous Parable of the Weeds. The emphasis here seems to be on evangelism, and the true fish which will be determined by God in His own time.

Explaining the Text	*Examining the Text*
1. Small fishing nets could be drawn right into the boat. Large nets swept the lake for as much as half a mile and had to be pulled by two boats to the shore. Obviously the nets contained all types and sizes of fish.	1. Read Matthew 13:47-52. To what is Jesus referring when He uses the phrase "end of the age"? (v. 49) 2. What might Jesus have meant when He talked about bringing out of one's storeroom "new treasures as well as old"? (v. 52) How does that apply to our Bible study today?

Experiencing the Text

1. Think about the four kinds of soil. Which kind are you?

2. What does the Parable of the Weeds tell us about how to handle people in the church whom we think might be unsaved?

3. Describe some ways you have seen the "yeast" of false doctrines grow in the late 20th century.

4. Review verse 42. What do you believe about hell, and how does that have an impact on your life and ministry?

5. Can you recall experiencing joy upon finding the pearl? How is your salvation like a fine pearl of great value?

6. Suppose someone asked you why Jesus spoke in parables. How would you respond?

7. If you were among the disciples that day, what other questions might you have asked about the parables?

STUDY TWELVE
Matthew 13:53–14:36

Motives of the King

After His busy day, Jesus went back to Nazareth and took His place to teach in the synagogue for the last time. Through a series of rhetorical questions, the people expressed their rejection. Jesus was forced to utter the common proverb, still used in our day, "Only in his hometown and in his own house is a prophet without honor" (v. 57).

The Herod of chapter 14 is Herod Antipas who ruled over a fourth of Palestine (that's the meaning of tetrarch). As the son of Herod the Great, Antipas ruled from 4 B.C. to A.D. 39.

The growing hatred of Christ took its toll in the execution of John the Baptist. But even though the forerunner went home to the Lord, the ministry went on. Our study concludes with the feeding of the 5,000 and the walking on the water.

A. QUESTIONED IN NAZARETH (*Matt. 13:53-58*). The attitude of Jesus' neighbors is a classic example of rejection. What is amazing is that the citizens acknowledged His wisdom and miraculous power, but denied that His authority came from God.

Examining the Text	*Explaining the Text*
1. Read Matthew 13:53-58. Why do you think the people of Nazareth were so reluctant to acknowledge Jesus' divine authority?	
2. Compare this visit to Nazareth to Jesus' earlier visit (Luke 4:16-29). How were they alike? How were they different?	2. Most evangelicals agree that the four names listed in verse 55 were children of Mary and Joseph born after Jesus.
3. Look again at verse 58. Are the miracles of Jesus always dependent upon faith? Can you think of any instances in which they were not?	

B. REJECTED AND JOHN'S EXECUTION (*Matt. 14:1-12*). These verses contain a retrospect passage beginning with verse 3. In other words, Herod had already killed John, but the reports of Jesus' ministry caused him to wonder whether John had risen from the dead. Herod had really allowed himself to get entrapped. Lust prevailed over logic, and John the Baptist was murdered in cold blood.

Explaining the Text	Examining the Text
	1. Read Matthew 14:1-12. Using a Bible dictionary identify which "Herod" is in view in this chapter.
2. Bible scholars suggest that Salome may have been between 12-14 years of age at this time. Herod's offer imitates the grandeur of ancient Persian monarchs (Es. 5:3; 7:2).	2. Study the text carefully and identify Herod's motive for putting John in prison.
3. Decapitation was practiced by the Greeks and Romans, but was contrary to Jewish law.	3. As you analyze this passage, determine who was ultimately responsible for John's death.

C. DEMONSTRATED IN THE FEEDING OF THE 5,000 (*Matt. 14:13-21*). The record of the feeding of the 5,000 is found in all four Gospels (Matt. 6:30-44; Luke 9:10-17; John 6:1-14). Jesus had been teaching and healing all day, and the disciples became uneasy about feeding the crowd. The miracle of multiplication fed well over 5,000 people, and from that time, believers have been encouraged by this demonstration of Christ's power and His care for people.

Explaining the Text	Examining the Text
1. Luke tells us that the "solitary place" was in Bethsaida on the northeast shore of Galilee (Luke 9:10).	1. Read Matthew 14:13-21. List three things we learn about Jesus from these two verses.

Examining the Text	Explaining the Text
2. How is the feeding of the 5,000 different from the changing of the water to wine?	
3. Do you find any particular significance in the coincidence that there were 12 disciples and 12 baskets of food left over?	3. Notice that Jesus gave thanks first and then broke the loaves. This would be normal behavior for any head of a Jewish household.

D. REFLECTED IN HIS WALKING ON THE WATER (*Matt. 14:22-36*). The disciples surely thought the feeding of the 5,000 marked the coming of the messianic kingdom. But Jesus made them get into the boat so He could go be alone with His Father. Caught up in one of those sudden storms so characteristic of the Sea of Galilee, the disciples were rescued by the One who controls all forces of nature. The trip ended at Gennesaret where once again great numbers of people came to be healed.

Examining the Text	Explaining the Text
1. Read Matthew 14:22-36. Why do you think that Jesus felt so strongly about getting alone to pray?	1. The phrase "considerable distance" in verse 24 suggests several hundred yards, probably out toward the middle of the lake.

Motives of the King

Explaining the Text	*Examining the Text*
2. The word *ghost (phantasma)* appears only here and in Mark 6:49.	2. What do you suppose the disciples really thought when they saw Jesus walking on the water?
3. Verse 33 is the first time Jesus is addressed by the disciples as the Son of God.	3. Contrast Jesus' words in verses 27, 29, and 31. What do we learn about Him and about the disciples in the progress of these verses?

Experiencing the Text

1. What lessons about prayer and meditation can you find in this chapter?

2. Consider the significance of the disciples' roles in helping to distribute the loaves and fishes. What might they have learned by this activity? What can we learn?

3. Why did the disciples seem to have continual difficulty grasping the reality of the person of Christ and the extent of His power?

4. How have you experienced the reality of the proverb, "Only in his hometown and in his own house is a prophet without honor"? (13:57)

5. What experiences are you encountering today that might be compared with trying to walk on the water? What causes your failure? How is it different from Peter's failure?

6. On what basis do you believe the truth of the disciple's statement, "Truly you are the Son of God"? (14:33) On works you've seen Him do? On blessings in your life? On miracles?

7. Write a brief paragraph suggesting how Matthew 14 will be important in your life and ministry.